Mapping Your Journey to Success
Six Strategies for Personal Planning

Mapping Your Journey to Success
Six Strategies for Personal Planning

Sharon A. Myers
Mark W. Wiggins

Copyright © 2012 Moovin4ward Presentations LLC

Library of Congress Control Number: 2012918888

ISBN: Paperback   978-0-9884564-0-2
        Ebook   978-0-9884564-4-0

All rights reserved. No part of this book may be reproduced or transmitted in any form or by any means, electronic or mechanical, including photocopying, recording, or by any information storage and retrieval system, without permission in writing from the publisher.

Published by Moovin4ward Publishing

Printed in the United States of America

To order additional copies of this book or for bulk pricing, contact
Moovin4ward Presentations LLC
1-888-893-6303
www.Moovin4ward.com
orders@moovin4ward.com

To book the authors to speak for an event, contact
speakers@moovin4ward.com

Table of Contents

Chapter 1 9
Planning for Success 9
- The Journey 9
- Six Steps to Developing a PSSP 13
Map It Out! 15

Chapter 2 16
Determine Your Destination 16
- DNA of Successful People 18
- True Meaning of Success 20
Map It Out! 22

Chapter 3 24
Identify Your Purpose 24
- It Starts with You 25
- Crafting a Purpose Statement 34
Map It Out! 35

Chapter 4 37
Set Your Goals 37
- Two Categories of Goals 40
- Set SMART Goals 41
Map It Out! 46

Chapter 5 48
Develop Your Strategy 48
- Plan of Action 49
- Personal SWOT Analysis 51
- Developing Strategies 61
Map It Out! 62

Chapter 6 64

Take Action 64
- Positive Attitude 65
- Hard Work 67
- Self-Motivation 70

Map It Out! 76

Chapter 7 78

Evaluate Your Progress 78
- Measuring Success 79
- Evaluating Progress 81

Map It Out! 91

Chapter 8 93

Law of Attraction 93
- Visualization Techniques 94
- Affirmation Techniques 99

Map It Out! 106

Chapter 9 109

PSSP Overview 109
- Action Plan Format 109
- PSSP Template 112

Chapter 9 116

Additional Resources 116
- Program 116
- Books 116

Six Strategies for Personal Planning

Sharon A. Myers | Mark W. Wiggins

Sharon A. Myers | Mark W. Wiggins

Chapter 1

Planning for Success

What a joy it is to accomplish something that you set out to accomplish for yourself and for your future. Many people do not adequately plan for success or prepare for the seemingly endless journey it takes to get there.

In this book, you'll learn the core concepts in success planning and methods to help you apply those concepts immediately and effectively. Our goal is to ensure that you've packed everything you need for your journey to success.

The Journey

So what is a journey? One definition states that a journey is an occasion when you travel from one place to another, especially when there is a long distance between the places. With that in mind, when you decide to take a journey, you must first know where you are and then the place you want to go.

So let's say we want to go to Barcelona, Spain. Every summer they host a huge carnival with an abundance of feasting, dancing, and partying in the streets.

You expect that this will be a trip of a lifetime, so you want to stay as long as you can and enjoy it for as long as possible.

The next step is to determine what it will take to get there. That's a long ride. It's going to be expensive. Are you sure you want to go to Barcelona? You ponder it and confirm that it's exactly where you want to go and you will stop at nothing to get there.

What do you need to do to make this happen? You know that you can't do it overnight. You'll need to make lots of arrangements and save some money. Your goal is to get there within the next five years. You decide to save at least $10,000 in cash just for the trip, because you don't want to do it all on credit. You want to come back from your trip smiling and debt-free.

Your plan is to pay off all of your current debt before you start to save the money for the trip. You'll need to get a passport. You'll need to find lodging in Spain for at least one month. You'll need transportation from the airport to the place you'll be living, and transportation to get around the countryside during your stay. You'll need to learn about the weather, so you'll know how to pack. And you'll definitely want to learn some Spanish so that you can communicate while you're there.

That's a lot to do and it can't all be done at once. So you build a plan that includes all of your "things to do." This is going to take quite a bit of time, energy, motivation, and sacrifice.

To make sure you stay on track, you may include a timeline of when each goal must be reached in order for you to make it to Barcelona by the date you've designated.

After all of that, you'll be ready to start working your plan: paying off current debt, saving money, learning Spanish, narrowing down housing options... all to make your dream come true.

Now along the way, unexpected things may come up. You might lose your job, you might encounter a natural disaster or a medical emergency that depletes your savings or you may not be able to get time off from work for one month. None of this is in the plan. In life, things, obstacles, and unexpected challenges tend to come along and turn well-developed plans upside down. But when you are committed, it means that no matter what happens, you are going to Barcelona. Why? Because you have planned for it and want it badly, that's why.

In many ways, planning a big trip is like planning for success. You'll need to know where you're going, why you're going, and then develop goals and strategies to get there. You'll also need to expect the unexpected and monitor your progress along the way.

What you need is a **Personal Success Strategic Plan (PSSP)**.

Developing a PSSP will help to initiate a disciplined thought process to produce a success plan which includes <u>making decisions</u> and <u>taking actions</u> based on who you are, where you are going, and why.

Keep in mind that *your* success is absolutely *yours*. You can't claim anyone else's, nor can anyone else claim yours. It's personal. So your plan will not mirror another and has to be specifically crafted for you.

Your plan should also be strategic... calculated, deliberate, premeditated, and intentional. No one stumbles upon success. People may stumble upon money, fame and even power; but this should not to be confused with being successful.

Being strategic helps you to work smarter, not harder. Just so we are clear, reaching success <u>does</u> require you to work hard. But working smarter allows you to better manage your time and energy, and allows you to anticipate your next step.

Thus, it is important that you have a PSSP.

Your PSSP will help to ensure that Barcelona is indeed the destination you want to reach and ensure that you've selected a destination that truly matches the purpose and vice versa.

For example, if your only purpose for selecting Barcelona is for "the huge carnival with an abundance of feasting, dancing, and partying in the streets" then Mardi Gras in New Orleans might be a more cost effective option to meet your purpose.

So "where" you want to go should match "why" you want to go there. Once the two match, you have to establish goals to help you get there (i.e. learn Spanish, save cash, pay off debt). Next you would develop strategies to help accomplish your goals (i.e. purchase Rosetta Stone and study 2 hours each day).

In the following chapters, you will be provided with details of the six simple steps to develop your own PSSP. "Simple" is not to be confused with "easy." Following through with a PSSP requires dedication, determination and commitment. Most importantly, following through with a PSSP requires self-discipline. Remember that you are going on a journey and the target is "success."

So what are the six steps? Let's discuss.

Six Steps to Developing a PSSP

1. Determine Your <u>Destination</u>. Once you've determined what success means to you personally, then you've determined your destination.

2. Identify Your Purpose. Your compass that guides you to what you want to do with your life is your purpose.
3. Set Your Goals. You need to have personal goals to which you can strive and which make it easier to take action and reach your destination.
4. Develop Your Strategy. Your strategies are the steps you plan to take in order to realize your goals. Here is where you detail how you'll achieve your goals.
5. Take Action. Creating a Personal Success Strategic Plan is the easy part, but is very meaningless if you don't execute the plan. Here is where you do the actual work according to your plan.
6. Evaluate Your Progress. Check yourself periodically to ensure you're still on track. If you're not on track, use the information gathered from this step to make necessary adjustments.

It's been said that "the journey of a thousand miles starts from a single step." Although this is the popular form of this quotation, a more correct translation from the original Chinese version would be "The journey of a thousand miles begins beneath one's feet." Rather than emphasizing the first step, Lau Tzu regarded action as something that arises naturally from stillness. Another potential phrasing would be "Even the longest journey must begin where you stand." [Michael Moncur, September 01, 2004]

Where you stand right now is in need of a plan—a Personal Success Strategic Plan. Over the remainder of this book, you will be guided through the process of developing your own.

Map It Out!

At the end of each chapter, we'll provide you with an opportunity to document your thoughts and notes on each chapter. We'll ask pertinent and specific questions to challenge your thinking so that you'll have plenty of information to use when you develop a draft PSSP at the end of the book.

We recommend that you take some time to honestly answer the questions or complete the exercises. If you feel as though you can't fully respond, you can continue to the next chapter and come back to it later. Or you can take your time to focus on your answer until you're comfortable with your response.

Keep in mind, you can always change and broaden it at any time. However, your journey to success begins with **making decisions** and **taking actions** towards setting and achieving goals to reach your destination.

Chapter 2

Determine Your Destination

Remember the game, "Pin the Tail on the Donkey"? Let's imagine that we have three participants playing. To win, the objective is to successfully pin the tail on the donkey. But in this game, the donkey is not on the wall and you don't have the tail. We know it sounds crazy, but go with us for a moment.

Player number one has been blindfolded and is wandering around the room aimlessly. The odds of this player even finding the tail or the donkey for that matter, is zero to none. Player number two has been given a map and is free to look about the room. Unfortunately, it's a map of the United States of America with no mention of tails or donkeys. Having a map is a good thing, but probably not very helpful in this situation. An inquisitive individual might consider asking someone around them for assistance, assuming anyone else knew the answers. This could eventually work; however, it might just take a little longer. Player number three has been given instructions. The instructions tell the player exactly where to find the donkey and how attach it to the wall. It then tells where to find the tail and how to pin it on the donkey. Done!

Surely it was obvious who would actually pin the tail on the donkey the fastest, if at all. But let's dig deeper and compare this game to life itself.

Let's say that by pinning the tail on the donkey, we've reached our life's destination. Like the first player, some people truly do wander around aimlessly in life. They have no clue as to where they want to go or why. Maybe they are blinded by the here and now, and have not thought about the future. Maybe they have not taken advantage of opportunities to educate themselves or build resources to reach their future. Or maybe they just don't care to live beyond their current place, because they are where they want to be. So they just hang out in life and do nothing.

Like the second player, some people have an idea of where they want to go; they just don't know how. They know they should be doing "something"; they just don't' know what. Many times, these individuals will have to rely on others to tell them what to do.

When we facilitate this game during our *Journey to Success: PSSP Program*, it is inevitable that someone will ask the audience, "where is the donkey?" Or they will simply follow the third player.

As in life, these individuals are asking, "Where should I go to school?" "What should I study?" "Where should I work?" "Should I ask for a raise?" Or these individuals will tag along with and/or follow someone else through life. Expecting that when the person they are following reaches success, they too can enjoy it. Again, this person may reach a destination, but they won't have a clue as to why they are there.

To be successful in life, it's important to define what success means to you personally. Your destination is your success. Once you've determined your destination, you can create a plan to reach it. Like the third player in our game, you want to walk thru life purposefully and directly to your destination.

You can do this when you have a plan that details, step-by-step, how to obtain the resources you need to accomplish your life's objective—your success.

DNA of Successful People

We all have goals we'd love to achieve, but the sad truth is that most of us will never achieve them. There have been plenty of studies done that show you how to achieve any goal. So what is it that separates successful people from everyone else?

Think of three successful people and write those names in the space on the next page. The people you list may be politicians, entertainers, athletes, or even family members.

1. _____

2. _____

3. _____

What do these individuals all have in common?

So what exactly is it that separates successful people or high achievers from everyone else? Believe it or not, it isn't ability or resources. It's hunger.

> *Wanting something is not enough. You must hunger for it. Your motivation must be absolutely compelling in order to overcome the obstacles that will invariably come your way.*
> -Les Brown

These individuals have a hunger to succeed that is so great that it fuels them to follow through and to keep fighting no matter what circumstances they face.

They don't get discouraged when their faith is tested. They know that doubt is a virus of the mind and therefore never entertain it. They are even resilient enough to persist and keep on following through despite what their fears might tell them.

Getting Hungry

So how do you reach a state of hunger for your destination?

<u>**You need to want your dream so badly that you'll perform at high output even when your faith is tested and there are no signs of success. And you need to be afraid of how uncomfortable you will be if you don't reach your destination.**</u>

Your purpose and your destination play a major role here. If you have a purpose that you care about and a destination related to it, you should have the hunger inside of you. If you ever think that you are losing your hunger, all you need to do is to connect again to your purpose and destination. Let them inspire you and bring the hunger back.

When you have these internal motivators driving you, then all you need is a well-crafted PSSP that outlines all the steps you need to follow to achieve success.

<u>**A PSSP is critical if you want to achieve your true meaning of success.**</u>

True Meaning of Success

In this chapter, we highlighted the need to determine your destination—your success. To do this, you must first define what success means to you.

While society has its meaning, which typically includes fame and fortune, that's not the case for everyone.

Remember, no one else can define success for you, so it's important that you have some idea of where you want to go in life or what you expect to be, for yourself.

On Feb 3, 1987, the New York Times published a research report on the power of positive thinking. On that report, Edward E. Jones, a psychologist at Princeton University said, "Our expectancies not only affect how we see reality but also affect the reality itself."

People often begin setting goals without a solid destination of what they ultimately want to achieve. But if you don't have a destination in mind, then you'll never know which road to take to get where you want to go. Your destination needs to be clear—something you can visualize and describe to others. Without a clear view of what you want in life, you'll be forever changing course and falling short of your potential.

<u>The best way to predict your future is to create it.</u>

Map It Out!

In this chapter, we highlighted the need to determine your destination—your success. Before we go any further, we need to define the **true** meaning of success.

Decision
_____

Jot down your answers to the following questions:

What is the **social** definition of success?

_____

_____

_____

_____

How do you **personally** define success?

_____

_____

_____

How does **your** definition of success differ from **society's** definition of success?

_____

_____

_____

Keep in mind that it is perfectly fine that your definition matches society's definition. However, be mindful that it's YOUR definition that you're trying to attain.

Action

Based on your answers above, take a few moments to describe, SPECIFICALLY, your destination. Keep in mind that it doesn't matter where you come from; the most important key is to determine where you want to go.

_____

_____

_____

_____

_____

Chapter 3

Identify Your Purpose

In life, we think we know where we want to go… our success, but when our success doesn't match our purpose, we tend to encounter numerous roadblocks and don't quite understand why.

Imagine you want to become an architect because your family has always told you that you are a great artist and should become an architect. After years of school and study, you determine that your purpose in life is to motivate children through art. While your destination was associated with art, becoming an architect is not part of your purpose.

As you continue through this book, we hope that you are able to give deep thought to what YOU want out of life—independent of what others think.

It Starts with You

You can significantly increase the odds of success in any endeavor, if you know who you are, what you want, where you are going, how you will get there, and what you will do once you arrive.

Your thoughts and attitudes have an incredible impact on your life. What you <u>expect</u> to happen often <u>does</u> happen. Because of that power, you need to personally define your purpose.

Let's seek to understand the "questions" that provide us with the "answers" that summarize WHO YOU ARE. Let's start with your personal philosophy.

Personal Philosophy

Every person has a personal philosophy, consisting of some rules adopted from one's parents, culture, religion, and environment and so on. Examples of these rules might include:

- Not consuming meats and becoming a vegetarian
- When and how you worship, if at all
- Not to smoke cigarettes
- Keeping pet dogs outside
- Using only recycled materials

Generally speaking, these rules are not always well thought out and contain a wealth of inconsistencies and contradictions.

Your personal philosophy answers the question, "What do I believe?"

Write four of your personal philosophies.

1. _____

2. _____

3. _____

4. _____

Legacy Statement

Your legacy serves as your life's defining statement. It provides an overarching framework for all mission statements and goals to follow. Consider the following deceased. What were their legacies?

- Mahatma Gandhi - peace
- Martin Luther King - equality, civil rights
- Steve Jobs – innovation, technology
- Michael Jackson – pop music, dance
- Princess Diana - charity

What legacy would you say the following *will* leave behind?

- Bill & Melinda Gates   _____
- Oprah Winfrey   _____
- Lebron James   _____

You legacy statement answers the question, "What do I want to be remembered for?"

Keep in mind that we don't always influence our legacy as we hope. For example, had O.J. Simpson died at the age of 30 we'd remember him for his outstanding football career. Unfortunately, most will remember that he was accused of murdering his ex-wife. His records as a football player have fallen to the way side.

Write a statement of how you would like to be remembered.

_____

_____

_____

_____

Mission Statement

A mission statement is a declaration of who you are, why you exist, and what you intend to accomplish.

You can't exactly choose what legacy you leave behind, but you can choose what you want to achieve in your life that will contribute to the legacy you leave behind.

Take a look at these mission statements:

- Al Gore: "... my goal is to share with you both my passion for the Earth and my deep sense of concerned for its fate."
- Oprah Winfrey: "To help women see every experience and challenge is an opportunity to grow and discover their best self."
- Charles Schwab: "... to help everyone be financially fit."
- John F. Kennedy: "... put a man on the moon by the end of the decade."
- Google: "... to organize the world's information and make it universally accessible and useful."

It answers the question, "What do I want to achieve?"

Write a draft mission statement.

_____

_____

_____

_____

Core Values

Our values act as our compass, guiding us through life's terrain. Values represent an individual's highest priorities and deeply held driving forces that motivate our actions. In other words, we make choices based on our values.

Here are a few examples of values:

- Ambition
- Competency
- Individuality
- Equality
- Integrity
- Service
- Responsibility
- Accuracy
- Respect
- Diversity
- Improvement
- Enjoyment/fun
- Loyalty
- Achievement
- Knowledge
- Reputation
- Democracy

- Courage
- Wisdom
- Independence
- Security
- Challenge
- Influence
- Learning
- Friendliness
- Discipline/order
- Generosity
- Optimism
- Dependability
- Advancement
- Authority
- Purity
- Stability
- Wealth

- Honesty
- Innovativeness
- Teamwork
- Excellence
- Accountability
- Empowerment
- Quality
- Efficiency
- Dignity
- Collaboration
- Stewardship
- Accomplishment
- Credibility
- Adventure
- Privacy
- Recognition
- Appreciation

So how do you know which are most important to you?

We can all glance at this list and feel as though most are equally important. Participants in our program had extreme difficulty in identifying which one is *the one* that drives our decision-making process.

So let's do a quick exercise to see which stands out.

- First, put a square around the 15 must have values.
- Now of those 15 in squares, put a star by the 8 that are very important to your well-being.
- Of those 8 with stars, imagine you are only permitted half or 4. Which four would you give up? Cross those out.
- Of the four remaining, which 2 could you live without?
- Of the final two, which do you care about the most… circle it.

The last one is your highest priority and it is one of your primary driving forces.

It answers the question, "What is important to me?"

We are certain that this was a difficult task. So, list your top three core values in ranking order.

_____

_____

_____

Code of Ethics

Lastly, let's look at Ethics. Ethics are a personal code of behavior. For the most part they will help define what you do with your life, the career you choose, whether you have a family, whether you marry, whether you become a CEO, or ... well, you get the picture.

That's because who you are defines your ethics and your ethics define who you are. It is a joined circle. Codes of conduct, personal creeds, and pledges all reflect an effort to make sense of things, to organize behavior, and to better understand ourselves.

Examples of personal codes of ethics:

- "I will maintain my physical and emotional health through regular exercise, good eating habits, and the proper care of my body."
- "I will continue to grow intellectually through personal study, comprehensive reading, and attending growth conferences."
- "I will manage my time well by properly balancing personal obligations, church duties, and family responsibilities."
- "I will seek to maintain a positive attitude towards all of my goals to reach my future."
- "I will be honest and responsible in my finances by paying all debts on time and not living a lifestyle above my means."

It answers the question, "How will I live my life?"

List three of your personal codes of ethics.

1. _____

2. _____

3. _____

Your answers to all of these questions provide fuel for achievement and are the reasons behind all of your actions and inactions.

There is considerable evidence to indicate that your expectations of the future tend to shape your future. It seems reasonable, then, to spend some time determining specific, worthwhile expectations that will make your life more meaningful.

You won't reach your destiny and fulfill your purpose until and unless you identify, support and empower who you are.

Purpose for Living

Deep within your consciousness is the realization that your life has a purpose, a destiny, a meaning to be discovered. To be working for a greater purpose, a purpose larger than you is one of the secrets of making life significant. Take the next 10 minutes to answer the following questions.

What are some purposes for living?

_____

_____

_____

What are some of the characteristics that make a "purpose in life" worthwhile and satisfying for most individuals?

_____

_____

_____

With those characteristics in mind, think about your purpose for living your life.

_____

_____

_____

<u>Successful people know what they want, how and when they will achieve it, but most importantly they know WHY they want to become successful at achieving their goals.</u>

Crafting a Purpose Statement

What exactly is a purpose statement?

A purpose statement is a sentence capturing what you're driven to be in this lifetime; it is an image of the future that you want to bring into existence.

To craft your purpose statement, you should give yourself enough time to create a statement that will really mean something. Developing your purpose can take days, weeks or sometimes even months.

Remember, you're developing this to inspire you, so make sure it is positive, upbeat and energizes you. Ideally, you want this to become an internal mantra that guides your behavior and response to every action and circumstance you face, so keep it short and sharp, up to a maximum of four sentences.

Map It Out!

As we stated earlier, you won't become successful until and unless you identify, support and empower who you are. Now that we have somewhat discovered who you are and your purpose in life, you can now more effectively identify your purpose. Remember that your purpose is your compass that guides you to what you want to do with your life.

Decision

Using the tips provided previously, take some time to draft a purpose statement.

_____

_____

_____

_____

_____

_____

Action

Once you have finalized your statement, you will ideally memorize it and use it to guide the formation of the rest of your PSSP, including your annual and monthly goals.

Consider, writing your final purpose statement on a blank sheet of paper everyday for the next 15 days to help commit it to memory. Remember that you want to do more than just identify your purpose, you want to empower yourself to pursue it.

Chapter 4

Set Your Goals

As the cliché goes, if you don't know where you're going in life, how will you ever know if you arrived? In addition to knowing your purpose in life, you also need to set goals to help you get where you want to go in life.

<u>Goals are an important fundamental element to developing a sound PSSP.</u>

Why is goal setting important anyway? How else can you hope to achieve your true meaning of success? Goal setting helps you to develop motivation and forces you to focus your time and energy. This helps inform what decisions you make in every waking moment.

When you lack goals, it's difficult to avoid just drifting through life as your day-to-day decisions have no larger purpose. Hence the saying, "If you aren't sure where you're going, any road will lead you there."

Setting goals makes life more meaningful and increases your level of positivity and optimism, ultimately leading to greater fulfillment and more achievement.

Your goals are different from your purpose. Your goals are the short-term desires that drive you to take specific planned actions, which we'll discuss in the next chapter. But you can have both short-term and long-term goals.

Many times, the short-term accomplishments help you to continue towards accomplishing the long-term achievements. For example:

A short-term goal might be to:
- Finish college
- Move into a larger residence
- Break-up with the person you're dating

A long-term goal might be to:
- Become President of the United States
- Visit 20 foreign countries
- Marry the person you're dating and have three children

So let's try a quick exercise to get your thoughts flowing on your short and long-term goals that you have in various areas of life. On the next page is a Goal Setting Worksheet. Take some time to fill in at least one goal for each category of life. It looks tough, but you can do it. This will hopefully help you to better understand the differences between long-term and short-term goals. You'll also need this information later when you are completing your PSSP.

Goal Setting Worksheet

Area	Long-Term Goal (5 years from now)	Short-Term Goal (1 year from now)
Career — Ambitions, dreams, hopes, etc.		
Financial — Income, spending, habits, investments, etc.		
Physical — Health, exercise, appearance, etc.		
Mental — Knowledge, attitudes, self-improvement, cultural, etc.		
Family — Relationship to others, role, education of family members, etc.		
Social — Relationships with friends, expansion of friends, community, etc.		
Spiritual — Spiritual commitment and growth, involvement with religious community, etc.		

Two Categories of Goals

When it comes to goals, there are two categories: "be" goals and "do" goals. In other words, who do you want to BE or what do you want to DO? Within each category, there are four basic areas of life: wealth, health, relationships, and self-fulfillment. So any goal you set for yourself will fall into one of these areas.

When a business professional sets a goal, it tends to be either a wealth goal or a relationship goal. However, achievement involves all four areas, and success means finding balance in the four areas. In order to live a successful life, you need both "being" and "doing" goals in each of the four areas of life.

Once you create a PSSP with your key goals you will find your life has more meaning and purpose. Eventually, you'll find that it's not just obtaining the goal that becomes exhilarating; but it's taking the journey and achieving the small milestones along the way to fulfill your purpose and reach your destination.

So, even though your purpose in life might be big, slightly abstract and thematic (for example: I want to be successful in my career, I want to be a good mother), your goals give you the opportunity to live your purpose in your daily actions (for example: I want to obtain Vice Presidency by June 2010, I want to spend three weekends a month with the kids.)

Set SMART Goals

Now that you know why having goals is important and the two categories of goals, you need to understand that not just any goal will do. You want to be sure that you set SMART goal.

SMART is an acronym that stands for all of the qualities and characteristics your goals should have in order to increase your likelihood of success.

In truth, we are all so resistant to change that we often try to sabotage our success. We'll not allow ourselves enough time or we'll not be specific enough in how we set our goals. Often we do this unconsciously and then end up failing and feeling perplexed as to why.

So what are SMART goals exactly? SMART is a system or a framework for judging the components of your goal. It stands for:

S	Specific
M	Measurable
A	Attainable
R	Relevant
T	Time-bound

Let's review each of these attributes.

Specific

Do you know exactly what you want to accomplish with all the details?

To achieve a goal, you need to be specific about what it is. Otherwise it's difficult to turn your vision into set tasks. To be specific, your goal should state clearly what you intend to accomplish. This will allow you to know exactly what you're working toward.

- *Bad example:* "I want to become healthier."
- *Good example:* "I want to become healthier by changing my diet to replace junk food with fruits and increase my workouts to three times per week.

Measurable

Are you able to assess your progress?

Making a goal measurable makes it possible to monitor your progress. It also forces you to become clear on where you're starting from, which is always important. If your goal is too undefined, you'll find it's impossible to tell when you have even achieved it. Your goal is measurable if you are 100% clear what success will look like and what failure will look like.

- *Bad example:* "I want to be rich."
- *Good example:* "I want to generate $100,000 in liquid income within 10 years of today."

Attainable

Is your goal within your reach given your current situation?

Research has shown that one of the most important elements of success is having a goal that's achievable. It's easy to get caught up wanting to do something HUGE. But the problem is: it's difficult to stay motivated over the long run if your goal seems unattainable. You will easily feel hopeless and abandon your efforts.

To ensure your goal will motivate you, break a really large goal down into smaller ones. At the same time, you don't want your goal to seem too small. The best size is one that stretches you without breaking you.

- *Bad example:* "I want to become a millionaire in 2 months."
- *Good example:* "I want to become a millionaire within 10 years by starting my own logistics company and winning government contracts to provide support in warzone countries."

Relevant

Is your goal relevant towards your destination and purpose in life?

A goal is relevant if it elevates you to your larger goals, your overall purpose. Remember that your goals are intended to help you to reach your ultimate destination, and therefore should not divert you from that achievement.

Let's say that your long term goal is to purchase a home and it will take you five years to save the down payment. But you decide in the short term that you want to take a two-week vacation in Las Vegas with friends. This will use up two years of your savings. It seems that your short-term goal is in conflict with your bigger vision.

- *Bad example*: "When I earn my degree in agriculture, I want to become a rap star."
- *Good example*: "Before I graduate with my degree in agriculture, I want to work an internship with a large company in the agriculture industry."

Time Bound

What is the deadline for completing your goal?

Deadlines are critical. They keep you in action and they keep you motivated. Without a time limit there's no urgency to start taking action now. Make sure you are realistic with your time frame. There's nothing less motivating than missing your goal all because you didn't allow yourself the right amount of time.

- *Bad example*: "I am going to work on my project."
- *Good example*: "I'm going to finish my project by Sunday evening at 8pm and I'll achieve this by working on it six hours on Saturday and six hours on Sunday."

Here are a few examples of SMART goals:

Goal	Promotion at Work	Graduate with Honors	Improve Your Health
S	Salary increase and new position	Graduate from college ranked cum laude.	Lower my cholesterol to below 200 mg/dl
M	Increase pay by 6%	Increase my overall GPA to 3.7	Decrease my cholesterol 40 mg/dl
A	Yes—each year three employees are eligible for a 6% pay increase	Yes—my current GPA is 3.4 with two semesters to go and all courses in my major	Yes—by changing my diet and increasing my exercise routine
R	Yes—getting a pay increase typically is followed with a position change	Yes—to graduate with honors, I'll need a minimum of 3.65	Yes—puts me at lower risk of heart disease and therefore, improve my overall health
T	12 months	2 semesters	6 months

To fulfill your purpose in life, you should set goals for each compartment of your life. You cannot separate family goals from career goals any more than you can separate physical goals from mental goals. They are part of each other, inter-related.

Map It Out!

In this chapter, we discussed the importance of setting goals to get where you want to go in life. You need to have personal goals in life to which you can strive and which will make it easier to reach your destination. Now take some time to develop your own "be" and "do" goals, then make those goals more concise using the SMART framework.

Decision

Take a moment to write a quick and brief (one to three words) goal for each category and life area.

	What I want to BE…	What I want to DO…
Wealth		
Health		
Relationships		
Self-Fulfillment		

Action

Now practice filling in each of the steps with different categories in our life to help us start practicing.

	Workplace	Education	Health
S			
M			
A			
R			
T			

Chapter 5

Develop Your Strategy

Goal setting allows us to be proactive, instead of just being reactive. However, goal setting isn't enough. Goal setting is just the first step to achievement. Imagine, for instance, that your goal is to lose weight. Knowing that goal needs to be SMART if you're going to have any chance of success, you decide you will lose 15 pounds by a date set four months from now. Time passes. Four months later, you get on the scale, and haven't lost any weight.

You shouldn't be surprised. While you started out well, by setting a SMART goal to achieve, you didn't perform any action to help you achieve the goal. What's missing from this scenario is a strategy to help you accomplish the goal you have set. Not having a strategy is like trying to pin the tail on a donkey when you're blindfolded. You don't have a chance.

<u>Your strategy is simply your plan of action to execute in order to accomplish your goals.</u>

Plan of Action

What will you do to make success a reality based on the goals you've set?

In selecting your strategies, make sure they are suitable for the goal you are trying to accomplish. If you wish to earn your degree early, skipping class is probably not a suitable strategy to help reach that goal.

Let take chess for example. Think about the goal of chess. The object is to capture the king of your opponent. There are a variety of strategies you can use, such as "bishop sacrifice" or "attacking F7". A chess player typically starts the game with their strategy in mind. The same can be said with checkers. The object is to capture all of your opponent's men or to block them from moving. Your strategy could be a move called "two for one," where you sacrifice one of your pieces to gain two or three of the opponent's pieces. A great checkers player will, again, start with his or her strategy in mind. We can even say the same with tic-tac-toe. The object or goal is to get three of your symbols in a row. Maybe your strategy is to take the center or maybe you like to start in the corner. Again, you start the game with your strategy in mind because it is your plan of action to accomplish your goal.

Let's say you have a SMART goal to lose 25 pounds in six months. What strategies or plan of action might you take to achieve your goal?

You may decide to join a gym, get a personal trainer, or consult with your doctor to change your diet.

Let's try one more. Let's say you have just joined a new student organization on campus and your goal is to become chapter president by the next year. What strategies might you take to achieve your goal? You may want to join a committee in the organization, attend all organization meetings, actively participate in events, or hold a lower level office such has historian or treasurer.

Be careful as you develop your strategies. Your intent is to develop a plan of action that will allow you to achieve your goal. If your strategies are not appropriate and suitable for the goals you are trying to achieve, then YOU'LL FAIL! For example, if your goal is to lose 25 pounds and your strategy is to stop eating, you will more than likely fail or starve to death trying.

You should also ensure that the strategies you choose are appropriate for YOU. There are likely more than one way to do something, but what works for others might not work for you. To increase your likelihood of developing strategies that will help you to achieve your goals, you'll need to create a Personal SWOT Analysis (PSA).

Personal SWOT Analysis

To develop your strategies, it's important to fully understand what makes you tick. Therefore, you need to understand the internal and external environmental factors that affect you.

With that understanding, you can develop strategies that highlight your clear advantages and use those to be successful. From there, you can make informed choices and implement your strategy effectively.

First, what is a SWOT analysis? It is a strategic planning method used to evaluate the **S**trengths, **W**eaknesses, **O**pportunities, and **T**hreats involved in a project or venture. Businesses use a SWOT Analysis to help develop strategies to accomplish business goals and achieve success, based on the capabilities and resources of the company.

	Helpful to achieving the goal	**Harmful** to achieving the goal
Internal origin	**S** Strengths	**W** Weaknesses
External origin	**O** Opportunities	**T** Threats

Developing Your PSA

To develop your strategies, use a PSA. Your PSA is a great tool for uncovering what you personally do well and where you have weaknesses, providing you take it seriously and dig deep. It's much easier to achieve your goals when your strategy uses your strengths without exposing your weaknesses and takes advantage of all opportunities available.

Once you've completed your PSA, take time to think about the different things you could do to create a clear advantage to meet your goals. **Brainstorm** on ideas then eliminate those that don't take advantage of your strengths. You'll also want to brainstorm on ways to maximize your opportunities, minimize your threats, and perhaps even turn your threats into opportunities.

With your destination in mind and the goals you have set in front of you, think about the possible actions you could take in order to achieve those goals. After an overview of each quadrant of the PSA, you'll have opportunity to begin brainstorming for your own.

Internal: Strengths & Weaknesses

The top two sections (STRENGTHS and WEAKNESSES) both originate internally. These are things that you can control. Strengths are helpful, weaknesses are harmful.

Strengths

Strengths are your internal, positive attributes and selling points. Develop a list of your capabilities and resources that can be used to help you achieve your goals. Then ask yourself, "What are my most important strengths? How can I best use my strengths to help me move forward?"

Here's what you're looking for:

- Positive personal traits
- Relevant skills, competencies, knowledge and work experience
- A solid education
- Strong personal connections
- Commitment, enthusiasm and passion for your field
- Extraordinary reputation
- Special expertise and/or experience

List of important strengths	What is the benefit towards your goals?

Weaknesses

Next, develop a list of areas that need improvement. Weaknesses can sometimes be the absence of certain strengths, and in some cases, a weakness may be the reverse side of your strength. Ask yourself, "What areas do I need to improve? How can I overcome my weaknesses?"

Here's what you're looking for:

- Negative personal characteristics
- A lack of relevant experience
- A lack of education
- No network or a small one
- A lack of direction or focus
- Damaged reputation
- Lack of skills or knowledge

List of critical weaknesses	How does it hinder your success?

External: Opportunities & Threats

The lower two sections (OPPORTUNITIES and THREATS) both originate externally. These are things that you cannot control. Things that are happening around you that may affect the outcome of your efforts to achieve your goals. Opportunities are helpful; threats are harmful.

<u>Opportunities</u>

Opportunities are external events that you can potentially take advantage of. In addition to new or significant trends, what other external opportunities exist and how can we best benefit from those.

Here's what you're looking for:
- Favorable industry trends
- A booming economy
- A specific job opening
- An upcoming company project
- Emerging demand for a new skill or expertise
- Use of new technology
- Referral to a high-powered contact
- Availability of training/education
- Lack of competition

List of opportunities that exist	What is the benefit towards your goals?

Threats

These are anything that can stand in the way of your success. No one is immune to threats, but too many people miss, ignore or minimize these threats, often at great cost or time loss. Ask yourself, "What can I do to eliminate each threat? Can a threat become an opportunity?"

Here's what you're looking for:

- Industry restricting and consolidation
- Changing market requirements
- Changing professional standards that you don't' meet
- Reduced demand for one of your skills
- Evolving technologies you're unprepared for
- The emergence of a competitor

List of critical threats	How does it hinder your success?

Getting Started

As you begin to create your PSA, be sure to be as specific as possible. Stretch to come up with insights. Take a break if you have to and revisit your PSA when you're fresh. You can even show your PSA to a few close contacts to get their views.

Then edit; deleting repetitive ideas and sharpening less specific ones. The intent is for you to use this tool to validate the strategies you can use to achieve your goals. This process helps you to understand your skills, attributes and experiences that you can use to your advantage.

On the next page are additional questions to ask yourself in order to help you get started.

	Strengths	**Weaknesses**
Internal	<ul><li>What know-how do you have that others don't?</li><li>What are you particularly good at?</li><li>What contacts do you have in your professional network that others don't?</li><li>What would your peers or colleagues say are your strengths?</li><li>What behaviors or beliefs do you exhibit that stand you apart from others?</li><li>Which of your achievements makes you most proud?</li><li>Do you have qualifications or training that differentiates you?</li></ul>	<ul><li>What part of your job (or previous jobs) do you dislike?</li><li>What are your bad work-related habits? For example, are you often late to meetings or do you forget to take meeting minutes?</li><li>What would your peers or colleagues say are your weaknesses?</li><li>Do you go out of your way to avoid certain aspects of your job?</li><li>What do your peers or colleagues do better than you?</li><li>Are there any gaps in your education or experience?</li></ul>
	Opportunities	**Threats**
External	<ul><li>What are the trends in your company, industry, or even the location which you work? How could you use these trends to your advantage?</li><li>Can you get access to tools or information that can help you in your role, or help you get to the next role?</li><li>Is there a problem or gap in the company or industry that you could fill?</li><li>Can you leverage your professional contacts?</li><li>How can you take advantage of what's going on in your company or industry right now?</li></ul>	<ul><li>Which peers or colleagues compete with you for the next promotion or position?</li><li>Could technology hurt your role or direction?</li><li>What barriers are preventing you from getting to the next step and can these be overcome?</li></ul>

Here are some sample **"brainstorming"** answers:

	Strengths	Weaknesses
Internal	- Excellent communication skills - Patience - Self-Discipline - Sense of Humor - Enthusiastic and inspiring - Creative/Innovative - Outgoing and competitive - Sees the "big picture" - Good at working alone - Good people/task organization skills - Cooperative & collaborative - Able to think on feet - Great qualifications - Knowledgeable about industry - Good contacts with community leaders - Friendly and approachable - Hardworking/committed - Organization skills - Customer focused - Strong follow-thru - Articulate - Ambitious	- Procrastination - Perfectionism - Harsh Self-Judgment - Poor organization skills - Poor detailed planning skills - Poor computer skills - Can be difficult to manage - Easily bored with routine work - Impatient - Work life balance - Listening - Repeating myself - Confidence in work - Arrogant
	Opportunities	Threats
External	- New career direction - New challenges - Wider career prospects - Experience in a different environment - Fewer restraints - No rigid career progression - Better earning prospects - More autonomy - Put degree skills into practice - Self employment	- No specific training qualifications - No commercial experience - No experience in private sector - Too many more qualified competitors - No management experience - Unused to working in a variety of environments - Too much competition - Technology changes - Recession

Here are some sample **"complete sentence"** answers:

	Strengths	Weaknesses
Internal	<ul><li>I'm excellent at analyzing problems and deciding the way forward.</li><li>I have a good academic background.</li><li>I have traveled extensively and have a good understanding and empathy for different cultures.</li><li>I have excellent working relationships with my peers.</li><li>I have a better understanding of my competitors than my peers.</li></ul>	<ul><li>When I get stressed, I tend not to analyze all the options before making a decision and "jump right in" to what feels right.</li><li>I tend to be stubborn and unwilling to change my mind once I have made a decision.</li><li>Compulsiveness sometimes causes me to begrudge being given tasks.</li><li>Time pressure causes stress and can lead to emotional "hijacking".</li><li>I do not handle multiple immediately competing demands well.</li></ul>
	Opportunities	**Threats**
External	<ul><li>To engage others in providing feedback about their experience with me.</li><li>To receive coaching in service of improving my leadership skills.</li><li>To learn from others in similar roles to mine.</li><li>To enhance my ability to manage the need to complete tasks quickly in order to be able to deliberate more carefully.</li></ul>	<ul><li>The technology at which I'm skilled is becoming obsolete.</li><li>Despite being great at problem solving, I'm often very busy which doesn't give me any time to do what I'm good at.</li><li>Time pressure, which can derail my plan for self-improvement because it catapults me back to my "usual" habits.</li></ul>

Here are five tips to help you to develop a successful PSA:

1. **Be specific.** Avoid gray areas, vague descriptions or fuzzy definitions.
2. **Be objective.** Ask for input from others who know you well and compare.

3. **Be realistic.** Use a down-to-earth perspective to evaluate your internal attributes.
4. **Apply context.** Distinguish between where you actually are and where you can be.
5. **Short and simple.** Avoid needless complexity and over-analysis.

Developing Strategies

Now that you have your PSA, take a look at your goals and develop strategies to achieve them. Here are some examples of suitable strategies:

Goals	Strategies
Get a promotion and pay raise.	- Completing all assignments on time - Leading committees - Taking on additional projects - Develop relationships with direct reports
Graduate with honors.	- Create a vigorous study schedule - Meet with professors - Request extra credit work - Participate in study groups
Improve my health.	- Replace unhealthy foods with healthy foods - Develop an exercise routine - Visit my doctor more regularly for physicals - Take vitamins
Start your own business.	- Research the industry - Create a competitive analysis - Write a business plan - Identify funding sources

To be successful, you need to make things happen, not just let things happen.

Map It Out!

In this chapter, we stressed the importance having a plan of action---a **strategy**. Let's begin by producing a PSA below, and then list strategies to achieve the SMART goals you set.

Decision

	Strengths	Weaknesses
Internal		
External	Opportunities	Threats

Action

Use the information that you included in your PSA, develop strategies to achieve your goals. Make sure you maximize your strengths, minimize your weaknesses, leverage your opportunities, and eliminate the threats.

Goals	Strategies

Chapter 6

Take Action

You have now determined your destination, aligned it with your purpose, set your goals and developed strategies to achieve them.

Now it's time to get moving… **take action and make it happen**. There are three key components needed to get you going.

They are:

1. Positive Attitude
2. Hard Work
3. Self-Motivation

You need to have and maintain these qualities in order to persevere to your final destination.

Positive Attitude

Let's start with a Positive Attitude. There are so many benefits of a positive attitude.

For starters, a positive attitude will give you a heightened sense of well being and it will help cure any self esteem problem you might have.

But that's only the beginning. Read any book by Jack Canfield and you'll quickly learn that the quality of your attitude dictates what you can attract into your life. Esther and Jerry Hicks sum it up nicely in their book *Money and The Law of Attraction:*

> *"There is nothing more detrimental to your ability to positively attract than a negative attitude toward yourself."*

So if you're wondering why that thing you really want just won't make its way into your life despite the fact you have a plan in place to attract it, consider it's your attitude that's blocking the way.

In his books, *Creating Health* and *Creating Affluence,* Deepak Chopra discusses the impact of the mind on the body. He believes that a positive attitude leads to the release of chemicals and hormones that promote optimal health.

Basically, a positive attitude is so powerful you can think of it as the foundation for allowing abundance of all kind into your life.

Considering the many benefits of a positive attitude, why aren't more people positive? The reality is that we are socialized to be cynical and lazy. We're programmed to blame everyone else (especially our parents!) for all that's going wrong in our lives. We seek out jobs that will give us the highest pay for the least amount of work, never considering what will lead to satisfaction and happiness.

And should someone say "change your attitude", they risk getting a "beat down". We're all so convinced that our own private struggles are so huge that we have good reason to be negative and therefore think small.

Most people think they have a positive attitude. But many don't. Someone who uses the power of a positive attitude isn't swayed by negative circumstances. They see them as minor speed bumps in their journey.

If you are serious about creating a successful life for yourself, you need to start by cultivating the right attitude. Remember too that it's easy to have a positive attitude when everything is working the way you want it to.

The biggest challenge is keeping a positive attitude when times are difficult. And most successes will require difficult times. If you can survive through the challenges, you'll be a changed person.

"Strength and growth come only through continuous effort and struggle."
- Napoleon Hill

Whether or not you have a positive attitude right now, you can adopt one. Remember, a positive attitude isn't a feeling. It's a state of mind. You develop a positive attitude by *deciding* you'll respond positively to life circumstances, no matter what.

There will be days when it's difficult to maintain a positive attitude, but don't be discouraged. You haven't failed, simply because you find yourself screaming at the driver in front of you that cut you off.

Again, what separates high achievers from everybody else is their ability to regain their positive attitude after they have fallen off the wagon. Be sure you get right back on again.

Most importantly resolve to start right now to be more positive. Always look for *how* you can do something rather than *why* you can't. Believe in yourself no matter what. And be disciplined enough to continuously seek ways to improve. If you do this diligently, in time you will start to experience the truly life-changing benefits of a positive attitude.

Hard Work

Not everyone who's on top today got there with success after success. More often than not, those who history best remembers were faced with numerous obstacles that forced them to work harder and show more determination than others.

But somehow, the world seems to be unwilling to admit that simple, good, old-fashioned hard work can be the basis of success.

Studies are constantly being made to determine personalities, hormone ratios, childhood characteristics, intelligence, education, methods, techniques, and the rationale of successful people. The fact that they work hard is shoved aside as some strange coincidence.

Thomas Edison tried futility for years to convince the world that his inventions were not the result of any great genius he had. "Genius is one percent inspiration and 99 percent perspiration," was the way he explained it. "I never did anything worth doing by accident nor did any of my inventions come by accident; they came by work."

He left, at the time of his death, some 2500 notebooks crammed with notes of his work and ideas. He would work himself into virtual exhaustion and then sleep on a cot he had in his laboratory until sufficiently refreshed to again pursue his work.

It would be difficult to argue that **Michael Jordan** wasn't the greatest to ever step on a basketball court (yeah yeah, Kobe this, LeBron that). But Jordan wouldn't have been Jordan without a lot of hard work, dedication and yes, failure. Practicing hours before school and not resting until he had eliminated the weaknesses in his game.

"I've missed more than 9000 shots in my career. I've lost almost 300 games. 26 times, I've been trusted to take the game winning shot and missed. I've failed over and over and over again in my life. And that is why I succeed."

You heard it told that **Michael Jackson** "had a gift," "he was born with it," or "he was lucky." But if the truth is to be told, he worked his butt off. What people saw on stage at his peak was a culmination of decades of grueling hours of dedication to his work and perfecting his craft.

His childhood consisted of him spending thousands of hours in the studio rehearsing, practicing, and ensuring he hit every note. He carried that mindset into adulthood, spending several consecutive days and nights in the studio to fine-tune every second of his individual records.

Walt Disney was fired by a newspaper editor because "he lacked imagination and had no good ideas." But he had big dreams. After a number of his businesses ended in bankruptcy and failure, he eventually made his dreams come true with a lot of vision, planning, and hard work.

And the list goes on and on. Visit www.onlinecollege.org and search for "the 50 famously successful people who failed first."

So the best kept secret of success seems to be that success, strangely enough, is always preceded by hard work.

Self-Motivation

Hard work and motivation often go hand in hand. Motivation is one of the most important prerequisites for achieving one's goals. People who are successful at reaching their goals have done so because they have stayed motivated.

Staying motivated when things don't go the way you want can be difficult. But keeping a positive attitude can help you stay committed, motivated, and inspired. Motivation is important to meet goals and finish projects. Some people may be very self-driven and others may need a high level of motivation to finish a task. It's very important that you know what motivates you personally.

Again, when you don't know what your purpose is, or you don't know where you want to go, it's hard to develop the motivation to go anywhere. Most people who live without a purpose get tied up in the day-to-day monotony of life, like paying bills, cleaning and just getting by.

When you have a larger purpose, you elevate yourself above these concerns. Yes, they're still important and you still have to do them, but your focus is on something much bigger. So first things first: make sure you are sure of what your purpose is before you look to motivate yourself. Otherwise, you'll quickly find yourself back here looking for new self-motivation tips, as the ones you try won't work.

Sources of Motivation

So it's important to examine what motivates you to move forward. Researchers have studied what motivates people and have identified two types of motivators: *internal* (inside a person) or *external* (outside a person). Most people aren't motivated by one or the other, but some combination of the two. Let's examine the two types of motivators.

Internal Motivators

When people are internally motivated, no amount of money, recognition, or other external item you offer, will be motivating. Internally motivated people are driven by how they feel about their own actions.

Here are a few internal motivations and examples:

- **Achievement:** The desire to achieve something, to work for the challenge rather than the reward, is the motivation. *Example: To participate in a 30-mile walk-a-thon.*
- **Competence:** The desire to master a job or do your best is the motivation. *Example: To learn how to use a software product.*
- **Belief in Something:** The desire to uphold personal values or ethics or fight for an individual belief is the motivation. *Example: To support animal rights.*

External Motivators

When people are externally motivated, it's what they can get that motivates them to do or continue doing something. Externally motivated people are driven to act by money, material goods, being promoted, or receiving recognition.

Here are a few external motivations and examples:

- **Power:** The desire to seek control or have your opinions drive what others do is the motivation. *Example: To be the one who chooses which design to use for invitations to an annual event.*
- **Affiliation:** The desire to be with other people while accomplishing certain goals is the motivation. *Example: To work with the kids in the class who like science the most on a group project.*
- **Position:** The desire to "move up the ladder" in a group to the top position is the motivation. *Example: To be shift manager at a part-time job.*
- **Hero:** The desire to do well in the eyes of someone you admire or respect, or to be like that person, is the motivation. *Example: To show your coach you can do your best time ever at the final season competition.*

Staying Motivated

It's an expected part of any journey of value that you'll lose motivation at some point. Real journeys are transformational. They change who you are as you travel on your journey. And a loss of motivation usually occurs right before a significant shift is set to take place.

Staying motivated is a struggle... our drive is constantly assaulted by negative thoughts and anxiety about the future. Everyone faces doubt and depression. What separates the highly successful is the ability to keep moving forward.

There is no simple solution for a lack of motivation. Even after beating it, the problem reappears at the first sign of failure. The key is understanding that your thoughts and how they drive your emotions. By learning how to nurture motivating thoughts, neutralize negative ones, and focus on the task at hand, you can pull yourself out of a slump before it gains momentum.

Here are a few tips to help you stay motivated:

Face your fears

Often fear can cripple your energy and stop you from feeling motivated. When this happens, remind yourself that fear is just a feeling, and an irrational one at that. Then face your fear. You will feel more motivated once you face and conquer it.

Seek out role models

Read about people who've achieved what you want to achieve. There's nothing more powerful than knowing someone else has done what you so badly want to do. Seek out biographies on people who've fought and overcome their own hurdles. You might be surprised at how similar your challenges are to the ones they faced.

Change your perspective

Often when we face hurdles we feel defeated and want to give in. If you remind yourself at these times that every meaningful success involves many challenges, then you will suddenly see that your current challenge is in fact a sign of progress; it's all in how you look at it.

Finish what you start

Consider making this one of your codes of ethics. When you are faced with a loss of motivation, remind yourself that if you don't finish what you start you'll be breaking the rules you live by.

Take risks

A loss of motivation can come when we feel paralyzed in having to do something outside of our comfort zone. When you're taking risks, or daring yourself to do something out of the box, you feel invigorated and energized.

And finally, the most powerful of all the self-motivation tips:

<u>Always go big… or go home</u>

If you're going do something, DO IT! If you don't you might find life feels hollow and empty. Achieve your success by reaching your destination!

> *"If you deliberately plan on being less than you are capable of being, then I warn you that you'll be unhappy for the rest of your life." –Abraham Maslow*

When you're doing what you love or going after what you truly desire you'll struggle much less frequently with how to develop motivation. And the only time, if ever, that you'll need some outside help is when you're managing your resistance to change (i.e. your ego).

Map It Out!

In this chapter, we challenged you to TAKE ACTION and work your plan. We provided you with techniques on keeping a positive attitude, examples of working hard, and tips on staying motivated. Since motivation is the key to having a positive attitude and working hard, let's take a deeper look at what truly motivates you.

Decision

How often do you think about what motivates you?

Most people only think about it when they start a new project or set a new goal.

Knowing how and why you get motivated can help you understand how to stay on track towards achieving your goals.

Read the following 20 specific sources of motivation or motivators on the next page.

Rank the items from most to least important (start with 1 being the most important).

	Respecting and valuing the culture and background of others		Being respected or having others look up to me or ask for my advice
	Having a job that pays well		Being noticed or having girls or guys like me
	Being selected for a new position		Doing the right thing
	Having family approval		Following through on responsibilities and commitments
	Being seen as a good person		Learning new things
	Having food		Getting a compliment
	Being able to do things my way		Participating in community activities to help others
	Owning stuff, such as brand-name clothes, shoes, electronics, etc		Having someone to look up to
	Achieving a goal I set for myself		Believing in a cause and standing up for what I believe in
	Partying or being social		Enjoying what I am doing

Circle your five strongest motivators and put two circles around your weakest.

Action

If your top 5 motivators were taken away, what would you do to motivate yourself?

___

___

In everyday situations, do you think about what motivates you? Why or why not?

___

___

Chapter 7

Evaluate Your Progress

Although you have determined your destination, identified your purpose, created great goals, and developed your strategies… your PSSP is not complete until you have outlined your plan to evaluate your progress along your journey.

For example, have you ever gone on a trip to visit someone for the first time and were given landmarks? Consider these landmarks as your milestones, your short-term goals that you must accomplish before you reach your final destination. Every landmark that you spot, is a goal achieved.

If you planned to reach one of these goals within a certain time frame *and you don't*, then you need to stop and determine where you are and how far you are away. Did you miss a turn? Are you going in the right direction? Once you've identified how far you are off course, make the appropriate adjustments to get back on track.

Keep in mind that you are on a *journey*... to success. Even with a GPS to guide you on your way—your PSSP—there will always be some unforeseen encounters. Some roads that you plan to travel will be under construction, so you'll need to expect detours, decreased speed limits, and roadblocks along the way. Take these opportunities to evaluate your progress. The process of reflection and evaluation allows us to ask, "Am I there yet?" and "Am I still on track and on schedule?"

Measuring Success

We discussed in Chapter 6 that there is no shortcut to success, except for hard work. To be successful in what you do you need to prioritize your work and take one task at a time. Believing in yourself and keeping yourself motivated and determined to achieve your goals will go a long way in helping you to enjoy success.

Just as the definition of the word "success" is different for everybody, so is the means to evaluate it.

So how exactly do you measure success?

Take a moment to answer the questions in the following table with "agree" or "disagree". Place a checkmark in the appropriate column and then write an explanation for your choice.

How do you measure success?	Agree	Disagree
1. Success is measured by wealth, fame and power. Unless you have those three things, you are not successful.		
2. Success is measured by happiness. If you are not happy in your life, then you are not successful.		
3. Success can only be measured by your parents. If you fulfill the wishes and dreams of your parents, you are successful.		
4. Since success is the opposite of failure, you are successful only when you don't fail.		
5. Success can only be measured by achieved goals. If you have not reached any goals, you are not successful.		
6. Success cannot be measured because it is a continuous and ever-lasting process.		

So let's go back to our original question, "how do you measure success?" There is no best answer for this question. Success is personal. Once you define what it means to you, you will be able to <u>evaluate</u> your progress towards it, based on *your* personal definition.

Evaluating Progress

So how do you *evaluate* your progress?

You evaluate your progress by tracking your completion of goals using the *Progress Evaluation Process*™ or *PEP*. The PEP asks specific questions to help you determine where you are within your journey.

There are three primary questions and six actions involved in the PEP. These are your critical milestones. Your answers to these questions will help you to evaluate your progress and take the necessary actions to keep you moving forward.

Let's take a quick look at the PEP flowchart on the next page and the description of the steps within the process.

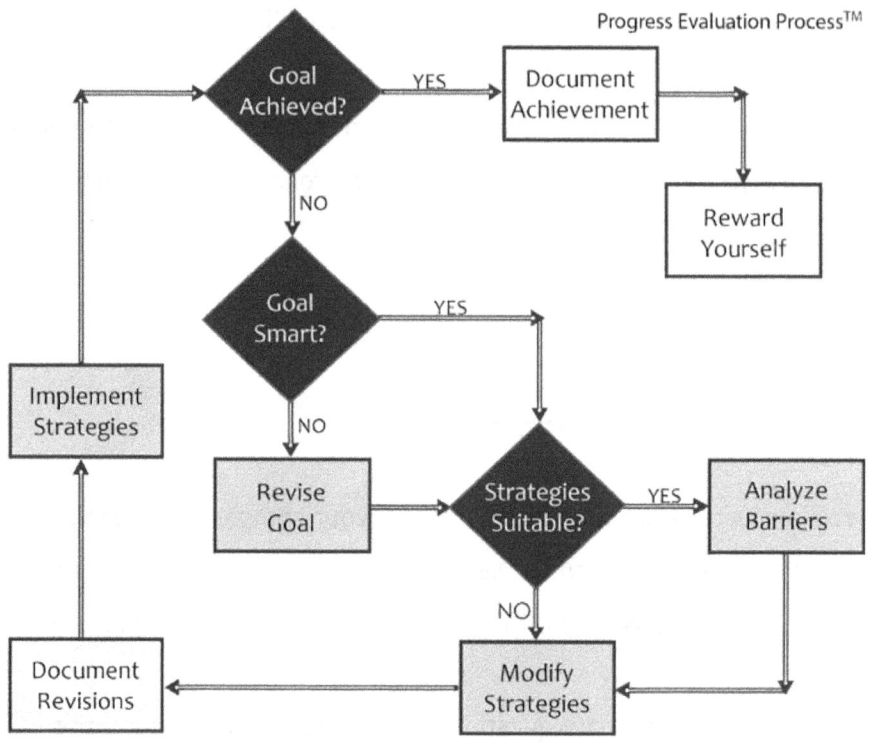

The first question is, *"Did you achieve your goal?"* If you did achieve your goal, **document** your accomplishment in your PSSP and then **reward yourself.** If your goal was not achieved, ask yourself the second question, *"Was my goal a SMART goal?"* Review the goal to ensure that you accurately used the SMART framework that was discussed in Chapter 4. If the goal is not SMART, **revise the goal**. If the goal was SMART and/or you revised the goal to ensure it was SMART, ask yourself the final question, *"Were my strategies suitable for the goal?"* Review the strategies assigned to the goal and determine whether the strategies are all appropriate to help you accomplish the goal. If not, **modify the strategies.**

If the strategies are indeed fitting, then you'll need to **analyze the potential barriers** that may be hindering you from accomplishing the goals. Once the barriers have been identified and removed, modify your strategies to accommodate your expected results. The next action is to **document all revisions** to goals and strategies in your PSSP. Now it's time to once again **implement the strategies**.

Let's discuss the actions involved in the PEP in more detail.

1. Reward Yourself
2. Review & Revise Goals
3. Review & Revise Strategies
4. Analyze & Remove Barriers
5. Update PSSP & Implement Strategies
6. Documentation

Reward Yourself

Let's talk about those rewards.

If you still wonder how to stay motivated, then note that rewarding yourself with every small success, with every small achievement, is very essential. Most of us want and need to be rewarded for our achievements. With rewards, you can be motivated and start working with renewed inspiration and passion towards your success!

Promise yourself a reasonable reward once you have achieved your goal. Let the idea of the tantalizing reward become your source of motivation. Your self-motivation will increase enormously if you give yourself a pat on the back for a job well done. Your reward doesn't have to cost a lot. In fact, it doesn't have to cost anything, i.e. lounging and watching your favorite television show, working on your favorite hobby or enjoying some music. Therefore, rewarding is one of the best self-motivation strategies.

Review & Revise Goals

One of the reasons why you may not have achieved your goal is because you did not accurately use the SMART framework to establish that goal. So the first thing you'll want to do is ensure is that your goal is indeed specific, measurable, attainable, relevant and time-bound, as discussed in Chapter 4.

While you are reassessing your goals be mindful that you don't want to set goals that are harmful to you. For example, setting a goal to stop eating to lose weight can be destructive. You also want to be careful to not set goals that are contradicting to others, or to set wrong goals altogether.

If you find that your goals are indeed good goals, continue with the PEP to the next step. Otherwise, make the necessary revisions to your PSSP and start again.

Review & Revise Strategies

The next step is to review the strategies assigned to the goal and determine whether the strategies are all effective and productive to help you accomplish the goal. For example, let's say that your goal is to get a promotion as work. One of your strategies is to take the lead on several work projects. This is a fitting strategy. Unfortunately, with the additional tasks you are unable to accomplish any one project because you are overloaded. Being unproductive will likely not help you earn that promotion.

Again, if the strategies are not suitable, modify them. If the strategies are indeed fitting, then continue to the next step. Otherwise, make the necessary revisions to your PSSP and start again.

Analyze & Remove Barriers

Let's say, you've set SMART goals and your strategies are suitable to help you achieve those goals, yet you still aren't making much progress towards your success; you may need to analyze the barriers that may be in the way. Below are the primary reasons that people experience failure in achieving goals.

1. Frustration
2. Over planning
3. Too much talking
4. Fear of Failure/Success

5. Feeling Overloaded
6. Unsupportive people
7. Lack of commitment

So let's discuss a few techniques on how you can navigate around these barriers.

Navigating Frustration

Sometimes you work hard trying to achieve your goal and all goes well. But sometimes it is frustrating especially when setbacks occur. The solution for dealing with this problem is to first, NOT beat yourself up. Second, you should divert your attention to how you can benefit from the setbacks. Be sure to not set goals that highlight your weaknesses or you will create new frustrations and possibly additional setbacks.

Navigating Over-planning

Too much planning can be counter-productive. It is easy to do, but you need to realize what actually helps you achieve your goal is *taking action*. Action is acting upon your goals and NOT keeping yourself busy. Keeping busy on unproductive tasks, such as planning and redoing plans, is an utter waste of time. Focus on the most important things if you want to get results... **taking action** to your plans.

Navigating Too Much Talking

Talking about your plans can also be counter-productive. Announcing your plan to others satisfies your self-identity just enough that you're less motivated to do the hard work needed. In 1933, W. Mahler found that if a person announced the solution to a problem, and was acknowledged by others, it was now in the brain as a "social reality," even if the solution hadn't actually been achieved.

In other words, once you've told people of your intentions, it gives you a "premature sense of completeness." Unless you are sharing your plans with someone that will help to hold you accountable, try to keep your plans private until you have accomplished your goals.

Navigating Fear

Some people are afraid they will fail, or even worse, they may actually succeed. As such, they don't even bother trying to attain goals. Such people lack belief in themselves and in their potential. In their mind, if they fail, everyone will think negatively of them. And if they succeed, people will be envious and think negatively of them. So it becomes a lose-lose situation no matter how they look at it. But realize that you can achieve anything you set your mind to. Believe in yourself and your abilities and others will too.

Navigating Overload

Again, the only time you fail is when you give up. If you have followed the goal setting steps outlined in the previous chapters, you will know that breaking up your difficult or complicated goals into small, easy, doable chunks is important. When you do this, your plan becomes a 'checklist'. What happens when you start completing these mini-tasks? You build momentum and eliminate feeling overloaded or overwhelmed.

Navigating Unsupportive People

Take a step back and assess the situation. Before you consider someone unsupportive, ensure that you have been clear in communicating your goal. If you have, then you can take appropriate actions to deal with the situation. Depending upon the relationship, determine if you should take heed in their advice or ignore them totally. Sometimes your goals are just not in line with other people's goals; as a result they will try to drag you in another direction.

Navigating Loss of Commitment

One reason why people don't achieve their goals or reach their destination is because they lose their commitment. One great way to get your commitment level back up to par is to review your PSSP regularly. This will help to remind you why you are on the journey in the first place. Success comes when you are committed and driven to make it happen.

If any of these barriers are preventing you from reaching your goals, deal with them immediately and you'll soon be back on track to complete your journey to success.

Update PSSP & Implement Strategies

Remember that your PSSP is a living and breathing document. This means that as life happens, changes may occur. You may even get sidetracked and not progress as you thought you would. But when it happens, it's OK. If you review your PSSP often and are willing to make adjustments along the way, you will stay on course to reach your destination.

Documentation

The entire PSSP process is all about helping you to document your plan for success. Your PSSP includes your destination, your purpose, your goals, and your strategies, along with any revisions or modifications. It will also include the actions you've taken, your accomplishments and your rewards.

We all have our own stories of perseverance; how we've fought against defeat and found the strength to continue following our PSSP to achieve our goals. But when your journey is a lengthy one, you sometimes forget what you've accomplished. You forget how far you've come. Documenting is a key step because it allows you to track, evaluate, and measure your progress.

Once upon a time, before computers and apps, a voyager would document his travels in a travelogue or road journal. Consider your PSSP as your travelogue. It is your historical progress report.

Map It Out!

In this chapter we discussed the importance of making pit-stops along your journey to check the tires, refuel, and check the map to see how close you are to your destination. Of course there will be bumps and detours, so be prepared and willing make adjustments along the way.

Decision

What barriers do you typically encounter? Of the eight barriers discussed in this chapter, rank your top 3 barriers and provide a brief statement on how you'll navigate around those barriers to reach your goal.

1.
2.
3.

Action

Write down 3-5 "must have" rewards that you could earn that would keep you motivated.

_____

_____

_____

_____

_____

Chapter 8

Law of Attraction

The Law of Attraction (LOA) says that whatever you focus on and give your attention to, you attract more of into your life. What you think, talk, fantasize and worry about is what you'll manifest. Our goal with developing a PSSP is to force you to put that focus and attention on your **destination** every single day.

Although we've already given you the steps to develop your PSSP, we've included this chapter specifically to help you to think positive and believe in your goals without having any doubts in your mind.

According to LOA, the key to achieve your goal is to repeat the thought of your goal again and again in your mind and holding to the feelings of imagining as if you have already achieved it.

Creative visualization and affirmation in achieving goals are the two most popular techniques used by many people and recommended by the masters of LOA.

Visualization Techniques

The most powerful technique in LOA is visualizing the fulfillment of your goal. You must take a few minutes of your day to imagine that you have achieved your goal. Try to take a mental picture of the day of your success and hold on to the feelings that you will feel the moment you will reach your goal. Most importantly try to interact with the day of your success in your mind. Try to feel what it's like to have your friends congratulate you on your success.

Visualization is a proven technique for achieving goals, whether your goal is spiritual enlightenment or winning a race.

In their book, *Karate of Okinawa*, Robert Scaglione and William Cummins give some compelling evidence of why visualization is considered one of the best self-motivation tips. They cite a study by Russian researchers prior to the 1980 Olympic Games. Interested in understanding the power of the mind on performance, the researchers developed training schedules that involved different degrees of physical training and mental training. They found that the group which devoted the most time to mental training (and the least to physical training) performed the best.

Their results confirm the power and importance of visualization. If Olympic champions use it to help them be their best, then we all should probably take heed and do the same!

Our goal is to help you to incorporate some of these techniques in your PSSP to help you practice positive thinking and prepare you for your _journey to success_.

Success begins within and visualization is a great way to convince yourself you can achieve your dreams.

When you are trying to manifest your goals, you're essentially trying to change something about your current state of existence. And with any change, the mind resists as the ego perceives the unknown to be a threat to the balance that it maintains.

When to Use Visualization

Visualization is important when goals require long-term action. For example, if you have a lot of weight to lose, it's going to require a lot of time just following a seemingly dull and routine plan before you'll see results. When you consider that many people eat because they're bored, you can see why this type of plan makes achieving the goal of losing weight more difficult.

As we stated earlier, as human beings, we have a tendency to sabotage our own efforts. This is why it's important to incorporate visualization exercises into your daily PSSP. You only need to spend a few minutes in the morning and just before going to sleep, picturing your success.

No one starts off as an expert. Visualization takes practice. Until you get good at it, it may only be words or feelings that come to you. That's okay because the more you practice the easier it will become. Let me show you how well you can already visualize.

Imagine that you're going to a bakery to help make cookies. You walk into the bakery and the smell of fresh baked muffins and breads fill your nostrils. As you enter the kitchen, you feel the warmth from the heated ovens. You head over to the giant stainless steel refrigerator to get your ingredients and you feel the cool air on your face as you grab five pounds of butter and a dozen eggs. You close the door and head over to your workspace where the huge shinny stainless steel industrial mixer is waiting. With your measuring cup, you scoop a cup of flour from the bend to dump into your mixing bowl, the powders float up to your face and you fan away the cloud. You reach for two more cups to repeat the process. You unwrap the cool, but slightly melted and mushy margarine and dump into your mixing bowl.

Next, you scoop a cup of brown sugar, which feels like wet sand when it touches your fingers. Next, you crack one egg at a time on the table and pour the slimy insides into your mixture. You repeat this process until you've used all of the eggs. During the process, you accidentally drop an egg shell in the mix. You reach into the mixture to retrieve the shell and you feel the slimy cold egg on your fingers.

Next, you add the vanilla extract. As soon as you open the bottle, the strong vanilla flavor hits you and almost knocks you out. You pour the needed amount into the mixture and now you're ready to blend.

You press the big green ON button on the mixer and it starts to loudly hum and rotate its blades, slowly mixing your batter. You stop the machine to pour in your honey and chocolate chips. You can't resist popping a chip in your mouth, oh the taste of chocolate. You start the machine again, it hums, and blends all of the ingredients into a smooth, creamy batter. With a big spoon, you lump moist dough drops onto your baking pan until all of the batter has been used and you've scrapped the remnants off the bowl.

Next, you open your preheated oven and the heat immediately moistens your face with steam. You put your cookie pan in the oven and set your timer for 15 minutes. After about 5 minutes you begin to smell the aroma of the vanilla, honey and brown sugar which makes your mouth water. Moments later, BING, the timer alerts you that the cookies are ready. You open the oven and again the heat blows on your face. After you place the pan on the cooking rack, you are tempted to try one. You know that the cookie is hot, but you pick one up anyway. The warm cookie begins to fall apart and you can see the melted chocolate spreading onto your fingers. You lick your fingers and take a bite of the cookie, which melts in your mouth and it melts in your mouth.

At this point, if you haven't already, you'll probably want to wipe your mouth, take a break from this book and go get some cookies.

The idea of visualization is to see yourself in it. If this visualization worked correctly, you not only were able to see it, but also smell, feel, hear, and taste everything that was done. That's how it works.

Let's look at the five things that go on when you are effectively engaging in a visualization exercise: (www.positive-thinking-principles.com)

1. **Internalize.** First, you need to see your goal in your mind's eye.
2. **Externalize**: Second, you need to imagine the situation when you've attained your goal, this time with your eyes open.
3. **Forecast**: Next, expand on the externalization. Play out a whole scenario in your mind. See how people behave towards you.
4. **Emotionalize**: Next, focus on all of the positive emotions you will have when you achieve your goal.
5. **Verbalize**: Lastly, picture your goals and the scenario you painted during your forecasting exercise. Say out loud what the scenario is that you see.

Creative Visualization

As we stated earlier, visualization is one of the most relied on self-motivation tips by Olympic trainers. Creative visualization is one specific style of visualization they often recommend. It requires imagining your desired goal by engaging all of your senses. The more vivid you make it in—bright, living, moving, color—the better.

For optimum results, use all five senses to work for you in reaching your desired goals. By combining the elements of sight, smell, sound, taste and touch to visualize your desired end-result, it becomes more real to your imagination and, as a result, becomes deeply embedded in your subconscious which, as discussed above, becomes your reality.

Practice visualization often, as much as three times a day. Have patience with the process as you learn.

Affirmation Techniques

Affirmations are a useful tool to help change the beliefs, images and thought processes that you have within you. It is a "self-talk" that affirms you positively or negatively. If you've ever said to yourself "No, I can't do this…" or "Yes, I can do this!" then you are using affirmations in both cases. An affirmation can either prevent or propel you from moving forward to accomplishment.

Affirmation is writing your desires or goals in positive sentences in present tense.

This technique has tremendous power to affect your mind in achieving goals, because you are writing and reading them at the same time, so it's like a double hit of energy. It works using messages delivered straight to your subconscious mind. If you repeat them regularly you can begin to reprogram your mind to have and maintain a positive thought pattern which helps attract your desires.

Basic Affirmations

Use basic affirmations to release the power of the conscious and subconscious mind. There are three statements that shape positive self-talk:

- **I am** – is a statement of who you are.
- **I can** – is a statement of your potential.
- **I will** – is a statement of positive change in your life.

I AM statements are positive affirmations of a real state of being that exists in you.

- ☑ I am competent.
- ☑ I am patient.
- ☑ I am forgiving.

I CAN statements are positive affirmations of your ability to accomplish goals.

- ☑ I can lose weight.
- ☑ I can let go of guilt.
- ☑ I can handle my course load.

I WILL statements are positive affirmations of a change you want to achieve.

- ☑ I will like myself better each day.
- ☑ I will graduate with honors.
- ☑ I will let go of past mistakes.

Once you've created your own basic affirmations, you want to embed them in the subconscious by repeating them at least three times a day. When repeating an affirmation, seek total relaxation. Then place the affirmation in your mind, and hold it there for at least 30 seconds.

Crafting Specific Affirmations

In an article by Shelley Holmes (www.qudrahealing.com, April 2, 2011), she lists seven easy steps to use to craft your own basic affirmations:

1. Be clear about the problem
2. Use present tense
3. Make it about you
4. Add emotions
5. Be positive
6. Be specific and brief
7. Be visual

Be Clear About the Problem

Many times people develop affirmations around the symptom of their problem, rather than going to the root cause. If you affirm a symptom, rather than the root cause of your problem, you may well find that you achieve results in the short term, but long term the results are not sustainable.

For example, you decide that you need a "graduate from college" affirmation, which is certainly achievable. But on a deeper level, the affirmation you really need is about going to class on time, completing assignments, staying on tasks, and studying properly. So you may need multiple affirmations and not just one to be clear.

As you begin to write your affirmations, ask yourself, "what is the real issue?" This may require a great deal of reflection, insight, and honesty.

<u>Use Present Tense</u>

Affirmations are more effective when stated in the present tense. For example; "*I have a wonderful job*" is a present tense affirmation. "I am going to have a wonderful job" is affirming something in the future tense, and even though it is only a subtle shift in the phrasing of the words, your subconscious, like an iPod, only records what you put in there. Therefore, by affirming "I am going to ..." you may well find yourself waiting a very long time for the results to happen, because you are forever 'going to'. Write the affirmation as if you have already achieved it.

Keep in mind that your subconscious is far stronger than your conscious mind and whatever your subconscious believes always becomes your reality. If you ever have found yourself saying "I don't know why I can't find a job that I like" it may be that your sub-conscious has a far stronger picture of your being miserable at work than your conscious has of you enjoying your job. This technique talks directly to your subconscious.

Make It About You

Your affirmation needs to be about you. So it will always include either the word "I" or "me" in it. You cannot make affirmations for other people.

For example you could not affirm: "My team members are open and honest with each other" - this affirmation will never change their behavior. However, if you were to say, "*I am open and honest with my team members, acting as a role model to my team*", then you may well find that your personal change will, strangely enough, have a positive impact on and may lead to changes in those around you.

Someone reading your affirmations may think they sound very self-centered and selfish. And that is exactly how they are meant to be; this is a self-improvement project. It might be a good idea to not share your affirmations with other people, particularly if they are likely to not support your efforts or put you down when you don't exhibit what you're are affirming.

For example say you are affirming "*I am calm and patient with the children when they are fighting*". Then the children are fighting and you find yourself shouting at them, your partner may well ridicule your attempts at shifting your behavior with "So how's that affirmation stuff working out for you."

Your partner may not understand that these changes do not happen overnight. But with persistence and practice, change will occur.

Engage Your Emotions

E-motion=Energy in motion. If it doesn't get you excited, it is not a powerful affirmation. So, get involved, be passionate, and use your emotions! Use phrases like: *I am delighted, I am so excited, it is easy for me*, etc. Bring your spirit and energy in to the affirmation - the stronger the feeling an affirmation conveys, the deeper the impression it makes on your mind and the sooner you experience positive results.

Be Positive

Create affirmations in positive terms while avoiding negative statements. Affirm what you do want, rather than what you do not want. For example: "I am never sad or depressed." What pictures does this negative statement immediately bring to your mind? Sadness and depression. Rather affirm, "*I have a positive and optimistic outlook on life*". This statement is much more powerful as it is positive and reinforces your desired goal.

Your words trigger in your mind emotions and feelings. You want your affirmations to be both positive and uplifting. A simple way to craft such an affirmation is to identify what it is you don't want and then ask yourself the question: "What is it that I do want?" Write your affirmation from the answer you get to this question.

Be Specific & Brief

Short affirmations are easy to say, and have a far greater impact at a subconscious level than those that are long and wordy.

Keeping them specific and to the point adds power and doesn't clutter your thoughts. If need be, have two or three affirmations around the one topic.

Be Visual

Now that you have written your affirmation, the key to manifesting what it is you want, is the process of vividly visualizing yourself as if you have already obtained your desired outcome. Remember, your brain does not differentiate between vividly imagined events and real events.

Use of positive affirmations on a regular, consistent basis will support your success.

Map It Out!

In this chapter we discussed the power of the Law of Attraction and two techniques that can be used together or separately to keep you motivated towards your success. **Visualization allows you to see yourself IN your success, while Affirmations help you to cheer yourself to it.**

Decision

So let's apply the visualization & affirmation techniques to help achieve a few of the goals you defined in the Mapping It Out section of chapter 4.

In the space provided, write down at least one visualization and/or one affirmation that you could use to reinforce your inner strengths and determinations to bring your goals into reality.

Remember, you are not required to use both LOA techniques, but the one that works best for you. For some goals, one technique may work better over the other and vice versa. Don't discount using both.

Life Area	My Visualization	My Affirmation
Wealth		
Health		
Relationship		
Self-Fulfillment		

Action

Every day, we all "speak" to ourselves, providing feedback on how we're doing. Usually, it is negative feedback. As a result, we feel worse and can possibly end up in a rut. By changing your "Self-Talk," you can actually begin to feel better.

You can reprogram your mind to enjoy greater happiness, wealth, confidence, love, success, health – and more; just by changing what you to say to yourself.

Practicing positive affirmations daily has a compounding affect. Affirmations alone, however, do not guarantee success… you also need to take action.

Consider either one of these two options to motivate yourself towards your success by using affirmations.

Option #1: Create several affirmations and write them on sticky notes. Place them where you can see them daily and be reminded of positive aspects about you. For example, you might place one on your mirror in your bathroom, on the dashboard of your car or on the desk at your office. Every time you see these cards, read your daily affirmation to remind yourself about your positive qualities and attributes.

Option #2: Write a single positive affirmation on thirty index cards. Take one card a day for each day of the month. This card is your affirmation for the day. When you get to the last card, start again. To make this daily affirmation process grow, write out thirty different affirmations for each month of the year. Keep the 360 cards in a recipe box and continually use the collection year after year, adding new affirmations, as you need them.

Chapter 9

PSSP Overview

Something magical happens when you write a Personal Success Strategic Plan (PSSP). Your desires go from being pie-in-the-sky daydreams to real and tangible possibilities. They then have the power to start guiding your actions and behaviors to bring them into reality.

Action Plan Format

When your goals are merely inside your head, managing any resistance to change is difficult if not impossible. But once they're on paper, you're on your way to turning dreams into reality.

This simple exercise of developing and documenting your roadmap for success greatly increases your chances of reaching the finish line. As you crystallize what tasks are required to achieve your dreams, you're programming your mind to prepare to take all the necessary steps that are required.

Now that we've covered all the tools needed, it is the time to produce your PSSP. All of the exercises you've completed provide you with a jumpstart.

Let's review the Six Steps to PSSP.

1. Determine Your Destination. It doesn't matter where you come from; what's important is to determine where you want to go.
2. Identify Your Purpose. Your purpose statement is a compass that guides you to the destination you've determined for your life.
3. Set Your Goals. You need goals in life to which you can strive and which will make it easier to take action and reach your destination. It is a necessary action that will keep you on your road to success.
4. Develop Your Strategy. Your strategies are the steps you plan to take in order to make your goals a reality. This details HOW you are planning to achieve your goals.
5. Take Action. This is where you do the actual work according to your plan. Your purpose statement will just stay a dream if you don't do this step. Be consistent every day in taking action.
6. Evaluate_Your Progress. Measure your progress in terms of your strategy. Monitor whether you are still on track in executing your PSSP. If you are not on track, use the information gathered from this step to take the necessary corrective action.

On the next page is the PSSP template to begin the draft of your Personal Success Strategic Plan. Use all the data from your notes throughout your reading of this book to map your answers to your PSSP. We recommend reviewing your information over the next few days to fine tune it.

You can also download an electronic copy of the PSSP at our website: www.Journey2SuccessPSSP.com/pssp_template.pdf

To test your skills and knowledge of the PSSP program, consider visiting our website to take the PSSP Challenge. If you pass, post a picture of your results on our Facebook page and we'll send you a free t-shirt. Just look for the "I AM, I CAN, I WILL" icon at the bottom of the home page.

Good Luck!

PSSP Template

This form is available electronically on our website at www.Journey2SuccessPSSP.com

Destination

What is my ultimate destination with my life? Where do I want to go? What do I want to achieve in life?

Purpose Statement

Why am I here? Who am I driven to be? Why do I want to reach my destination?

Goals

What do I need to accomplish to reach my destination and fulfill my purpose?

	Description	Category/Area	Resources Needed
1.			
2.			
3.			
4.			
5.			
6.			
7.			

Strategies

How will I achieve each goal? What is my plan of action?

Description	Goal #	Due Date

Actions

What did I do to achieve my goal?

Tasks	Date Completed

Evaluation

How did I do? Do I need to make any revisions to my goals or strategies?

Date	Revisions to Goals	Date	Revisions to Strategies

What are my successes thus far?

Date	Accomplishments	Date	Reward

In Closing

Remember that no one becomes successful by accident. Success requires making a plan and sticking to it. By following these simple steps we've outlined in these chapters, you can become successful and achieve all that you hunger for.

It's simple, but requires commitment; it's not hard to do, but requires hard work. The good news is that once you begin, the results start coming almost instantly.

The miracle of successful living is that the smallest step towards success attracts more success! Everybody experiences fear of failure, uncertainty, insecurity, low self-esteem, indecision, depression, nervousness and embarrassment. Successful people master these temporary conditions by taking positive action, by sticking to their plan, by maintaining their vision of the future, by learning from setbacks and by rededicating themselves to the pursuit of their purpose.

By following the six steps we've outlined, you WILL become successful in reaching your destination.

Success is Moovin4ward!

Chapter 9

Additional Resources

Program

The **Journey to Success: Personal Success Strategic Plan** Program Kit

- ☑ Formats include 1-hour, half-day, and full-day sessions
- ☑ Includes full-color program materials (worksheets & workbooks)
- ☑ Interactive with small group discussions, exercises, and activities
- ☑ Certified and Master PSSP Facilitators around the country
- ☑ Perfect for any audience

Books

My Vision, My Plan, My Now, Moovin4ward Presentations

My Now for the Entrepreneur, Moovin4ward Presentations

My Now for the College Grad, Moovin4ward Presentations

Permission to Succeed, Mark Wiggins

MTXE: The Formula for Success for Teens, Mark Wiggins

My Own Business: A Business Startup Guide, Sharon A. Myers

90 Tips for the First 90 Days, Sharon A. Myers

Index

Affirmation Techniques, 99
Analyze Potential Barriers, 83
Barcelona, Spain, 10
Basic Affirmations, 100
Canfield, Jack, 65
Categories of Goals, 40
Chopra, Deepak, 65
Code of Ethics, 31
Core Concepts, 9
Core Values, 29
Crafting Affirmations, 101
   Be Clear About the Problem, 101
   Be Positive, 104
   Be Specific & Brief, 105
   Be Visual, 105
   Engage Your Emotions, 104
   Make It About You, 103
   Use Present Tense, 102
Determine Your Destination, 13, 16, 110
Develop Your Strategy, 14, 48, 110
Developing a PSSP, 12, 13
Disney, Walt, 69
Document Revisions, 83
Edison, Thomas, 68
Evaluate Your Progress, 14, 78, 110
Evaluating Progress, 81
Gandhi, Mahatma, 26
Gates, Bill & Melinda, 27
Goal Setting, 37, 48, 88
Google, 28
Gore, Al, 28
Hard Work, 64, 67
Hicks, Esther & Jerry, 65
Hill, Napoleon, 67

Hunger, 19, 20, 115
Identify Your Purpose, 14, 24, 110
Implement the Strategies, 83
Jackson, Michael, 26, 69
James, Lebron, 27
Jobs, Steve, 26
Jones, Edward E., 21
Jordan, Michael, 68
Journey to Success, 17
Kennedy, John F., 28
King, Martin Luther, 26
Legacy Statement, 26
Map It Out!, 15, 22, 35, 46, 62, 76, 91, 106
Measuring Success, 79
Mission Statement, 27
Modify the Strategies, 82
Motivators, External, 72
   Affiliation, 72
   Hero, 72
   Position, 72
   Power, 72
Motivators, Internal, 71
   Achievement, 71
   Belief in Something, 71
   Competence, 71
Navigating
   Loss of Commitment, 88
Navigating Barriers
   Fear, 87
   Frustration, 86
   Overload, 88
   Over-planning, 86
   Too Much Talking, 87
   Unsupportive People, 88
Opportunities, 55
Personal Philosophy, 25, 26

Personal Success Strategic Plan, 12, 14, 109, 111
Personal SWOT Analysis, 50, 51
Plan of Action, 49
Planning for Success, 9
Positive Attitude, 64, 65
Princess Diana, 26
Princeton University, 21
Progress Evaluation Process™, 81
   Analyze & Remove Barriers, 85
   Documentation, 89
   Review & Revise Goals, 84
   Review & Revise Strategies, 85
   Reward Yourself, 83
   Update PSSP & Implement Strategies, 89
PSA. See Personal SWOT Analysis
Purpose in Life, 24, 33, 35, 37, 40, 43
Purpose Statement, 34, 112
Revise the Goal, 82
Reward Yourself, 82
Roadblocks, 24, 79
Schwab, Charles, 28

Self-Motivation, 64, 70
Set Your Goals, 14, 37, 110
SMART Goal
   Attainable, 43
   Measurable, 42
   Relevant, 43
   Specific, 42
   Time Bound, 44
SMART Goals, 41
Sources of Motivation, 71
Staying Motivated, 73
   Change Your Perspective, 74
   Face Your Fears, 73
   Finish What You Start, 74
   Go Big or Go Home, 75
   Seek Out Role Models, 74
   Take Risks, 74
Strengths, 53
Success Planning, 9
Suitable Strategies, 61
Take Action, 14, 64, 110
Threats, 56
Tzu, Lau, 14
Visualization Techniques, 94
Weaknesses, 54
Winfrey, Oprah, 27, 28

www.ingramcontent.com/pod-product-compliance
Lightning Source LLC
Chambersburg PA
CBHW070521100426
42743CB00010B/1898